LET *Heaven*
and
Nature SING

D1557605

"I keep hearing from parishioners about how much they love the Ave Devotionals. These booklets are rich sources of prayer and reflection and provide useful, down-to-earth spiritual formation during the most important seasons of the liturgical year. We are excited to share these with our people!"

Fr. John Dougherty, CSC
Pastor of St. Ignatius Martyr Catholic Church in Austin, Texas

"As a hospice chaplain, I am always looking for great prayer resources to offer those I serve. These books provide interesting reflections, relatable prayers, and familiar seasonal hymns that touch the hearts of my patients and their families. You can't help but feel comforted and draw closer to God when praying with these devotionals."

Margaret Manning
Hospice spiritual counselor in Springfield, New Jersey

"Weaving a rich tapestry of sacred music with thoughtful reflections and prayers, these little books invite us to journey in a fresh new way through the Church's most holy seasons, which are ever ancient and ever new. Whether it's your first or your fifty-first time through these holy doors of the Church calendar, you will find ample comfort, depth, and encouragement in these devotions."

Cameron Bellm
Author of *A Consoling Embrace: Prayers for a Time of Pandemic*

LET Heaven and Nature SING

DAILY PRAYERS

FOR *Advent* AND *Christmas* 2024

WRITTEN BY JOSH NOEM

AVE MARIA PRESS AVE Notre Dame, Indiana

Nihil Obstat: Reverend Monsignor Michael Heintz, PhD
            Censor Librorum
Imprimatur: Most Reverend Kevin C. Rhoades
            Bishop of Fort Wayne–South Bend
            Given at Fort Wayne, Indiana, on 25 April, 2024

Writer
Josh Noem

Founded in 1865, Ave Maria Press is a ministry of the United States Province of Holy Cross.

www.avemariapress.com

Paperback: ISBN-13 978-1-64680-356-9

E-book: ISBN-13 978-1-64680-357-6

Cover image © Linara Art Prints, www.etsy.com/shop/LinaraArtPrints.

Cover and text design by Katherine Robinson.

Printed and bound in the United States of America.

Introduction

The word *devotion* has its roots in the Latin word for *vow*, so the different shapes this word takes—*devoted* or *devout*, for example—communicate some kind of commitment and loyalty. A *devotional* simply takes that faithfulness and makes it accessible through a religious practice. It's a four-syllable word that points to the everyday, practical steps we take to grow closer to God in love.

If you're not sure how to go about deepening your relationship with God, you're in the right book! This devotional offers brief prompts for reflection and prayer to assist you each day from December 1, the First Sunday of Advent this year, through January 12, the Feast of the Baptism of the Lord. This season of remembering and celebrating the Nativity of Christ is a perfect time to anchor ourselves in God's abiding presence. It is a time to ponder God's nearness, for the One who came to us by becoming a small, frail child in a first-century family continues to come to each one of us. This movement by which God joined us by becoming fully human while remaining God is a source of profound wonder and joyful hope for us. The devotions of this book will help you cultivate these dispositions with music, brief reflections, and most especially prayer.

We will pray together in this booklet in a very Catholic way: with music. You've never seen a Catholic procession without a hymn for a reason—prayerful songs involve our whole bodies. Music engages our emotions: we use it to "lift up our hearts," as we say at Mass. Each day of this devotional opens with a lyric from a well-known Advent or Christmas hymn. A short reflection on that text follows, along with prayers for morning and evening and a simple spiritually focused question to think about throughout your day.

To help you pray, you can access a playlist of the songs featured in this book at www.avemariapress.com/let-heaven-and-nature-sing-music via your web browser or the QR codes that appear throughout this book (just focus your smartphone's camera on the box code and a link to this page will appear for you to click on). Each song used here has three or four versions available for you to linger over and pray with as you listen. You can find the complete lyrics for each song beginning on page 46.

Christ isn't waiting for Christmas to arrive in our hearts. Christ is with us now—in silence and song, wonder and joy—ready to enfold us in a loving embrace. Let us go to meet him together!

A ve Maria Press is a publishing ministry of the Congregation of Holy Cross, a religious order with a mission to educate in the faith by forming minds and hearts and drawing people into community. This book draws on the spirit that animates these priests and brothers—especially their devotion to the Holy Family, whose hopes and joys we enter into during this season. We were founded more than 150 years ago to honor Mary, support the spiritual needs of our everyday living, and showcase the best American Catholic writing.

Drawing on our Holy Cross heritage, Ave aims to set hearts on fire—and that's the aim and hope for this Advent and Christmas devotional. Thank you for being part of our family of faith!

Sunday, December 1

FIRST WEEK OF ADVENT

O come, O come, Emmanuel, and ransom captive Israel
that mourns in lonely exile here until the Son of God appear.

Somehow stepping into this four-week season often brings a small jolt of panic. Perhaps it's because we are thinking about everything we need to get done between now and December 25. The clock has officially started.

"O Come, O Come, Emmanuel" is the perfect antidote to the adrenaline spike and often-frantic hurry of this season. The pace is slow and deliberate—there's no way to rush through this ancient song. It forces us to be still for a few minutes and contemplate our own lonely exile. What keeps us captive? And why?

Prayer for Morning

Jesus, Emmanuel—your name means "God is with us." You share our humanity. Help me to see the ways you come to me—not in the abstract but in the real circumstances in my life *today*. Open my eyes and my heart to welcome you in the people and events that come into my life this day.

Ponder Today

Christ came to ransom us. What keeps my spirit captive? From what do I seek ransom?

Prayer for Evening

Jesus, Emmanuel, you come to me here and now. You are not waiting for me to get my act together or to prove that I'm worthy of you. You arrive in the midst of my mess and my to-do list and my regrets, for you want to share life with me. Open my eyes and heart to receive your gifts, O Lord, especially when I don't feel ready for you.

To listen to "O Come, O Come, Emmanuel," scan the QR code or visit https://www.avemariapress.com/let-heaven-and-nature-sing-music.

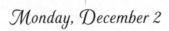

Monday, December 2

FIRST WEEK OF ADVENT

O come, O come, Emmanuel.

We repeat a phrase over and over in this hymn: "O come!" It might seem an odd invocation when we are preparing for a Christmas celebration of Jesus's birth at Bethlehem so very long ago. Jesus, the Christ, has already come into our world as one of us, so what are we really praying for in this song?

"O come" is a phrase that can carry our prayer today. Yes, Jesus has already come—and remains with us here and now. But this is our moment to invite him in deeper. "O come" is not a passive invitation—it is the pleading, welcoming command you give a loved one who stands outside your door. Our Advent journey is intended to stir up our desire to plead "O come, O come, Emmanuel!" and mean it because we long for him in every part of our lives.

Prayer for Morning

Jesus, you know and love me better than I do. It is so easy to forget this, however, and my inattentiveness means I often do not recognize you in the ordinary things of daily life. Stir up in me a desire for greater union with you. Son of God, I open my heart, my mind, and all my senses to you.

Ponder Today

Repeat the prayer "O come, O come, Emmanuel" today, especially whenever you run into a challenge or a stressor appears.

Prayer for Evening

Jesus, you are God's presence within and all around me. Help me walk with you through this Advent so I may grow in your love for me and learn to love you more fully in return. Son of God, deepen my faith and love.

To listen to "O Come, O Come, Emmanuel," scan the QR code or visit

Tuesday, December 3

FIRST WEEK OF ADVENT

Rejoice! Rejoice! Emmanuel shall come to you, O Israel.

Look at the lyrics of this week's hymn on page 46 and notice how this hymn is structured around a repeated call and response. With each verse, we call out for Jesus under a different title to come shape our lives—to ransom us who *mourn in exile,* save us *from depths of hell,* and give us *victory over the grave.* We plead, *dispel the shadows of the night.* Each verse is a new call for help: the words create space for us to express our own particular yearnings for God. Each is met by the unchanging refrain, seemingly uttered in another voice. *Rejoice! Rejoice! Emmanuel shall come to you.* This steady confidence is the faith carried to us by generations, those who tested life and found this hope to be honest and true. Across generations, believers have known that God is faithful and they urge us, *Rejoice!*

Prayer for Morning

Emmanuel, you come to bring us to our Father. Help me overcome division that weighs on my heart and form me to love as you love. Grant me confidence in your desire to come and shape my life. Jesus, I wait with ready joy for your coming.

Ponder Today

What signs do I expect will reveal Jesus's presence and lead me to rejoice today?

Prayer for Evening

Emmanuel, the gift of faith is handed on to us by generations of people who have known, loved, and served you. Help me to trust their experience of your love and, with them, follow you on our way to our heavenly home. O Lord, when I call, you respond.

https://www.avemariapress.com/let-heaven-and-nature-sing-music.

Wednesday, December 4

FIRST WEEK OF ADVENT

O come, O Wisdom from on high, who ordered all things mightily;
to us the path of knowledge show and teach us in its ways to go.

The trees of a forest communicate with one another through the fungi that share a symbiotic relationship with their roots. Trees share nutrients and information through this network of fungi to defend against parasites.

From the spinning galaxies to the invisible workings of the human heart, things are ordered. Wisdom is simply the right perception of this order—living in accord with it brings us harmony and purpose. We believe Jesus comes to us in the form of this wisdom; with this hymn we call to him, "O come, O Wisdom from on high, who ordered all things mightily; to us the path of knowledge show and teach us in its ways to go."

Prayer for Morning

Jesus, Wisdom of God, all things came to be through you and reflect your glory. Help me to seek your truth as a guide for my life—there to find the right way to live in your abiding presence. Wisdom of God, order my life according to your truth today.

Ponder Today

What is a belief you would stake your life on? How can that conviction shape your day?

Prayer for Evening

Jesus, you are the Way, the Truth, and the Life. You open a new horizon—one that draws me beyond myself into abundant peace. Grant me the courage to follow your truth, especially when it leads me. Wisdom of God, show me your way.

To listen to "O Come, O Come, Emmanuel," scan the QR code or visit

Thursday, December 5

FIRST WEEK OF ADVENT

O come, O Bright and Morning Star.

"O come, O Bright and Morning Star," we sing. *Dispel the shadows of the night and turn our darkness into light.* What does it mean to turn to Christ as our Morning Star—as the source of our light and heat and life itself?

Gloom covers us when we have no hope for our futures, when we dread night's shadows. Every reminder of our mortality—whether it's watching a loved one suffer illness or our own aching back or failing eyesight—raises the specter of eventual death. So we avoid it—we scramble back into the shadows where we don't have to face it or think about it. But God came to walk us through that darkness into the light of eternal life. We don't have to live in darkness—we can choose to live in the light.

Prayer for Morning

Jesus, you are the Light of the World. You came to share our humanity, even to the point of death, to reveal the Father's radical communion with us. Give me the courage to face the shadows in my life with the light of your love. O Morning Star, bring your warmth and heat to me today.

Ponder Today

What will remind me of my mortality today? How will I respond?

Prayer for Evening

Jesus, my brother, your light shines even in my deepest anxieties. Help me to embrace life with you as my salvation and chase away my gloom. O Bright and Morning Star, I look for your light.

https://www.avemariapress.com/let-heaven-and-nature-sing-music.

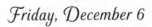

Friday, December 6

FIRST WEEK OF ADVENT

O come, O Key of David, come and open wide our heavenly home.

A key opens a locked door that we can't open on our own. We know Jesus opens for us the gates of heaven, but he doesn't just appear as a savior at the end of our story—he's acting in our lives to save us now. As Key of David, Jesus is the most crucial key to our existence as God's beloved sons and daughters. He is *the* key that closes doors on sin and death and opens doors that lead us to freedom and new life. He's ready to do that for each of us today.

Jesus explains he was sent "to proclaim liberty to captives . . . and let the oppressed go free" (Lk 4:18). This is not only what he *does*; it's who he *is*—he is the Key who unlocks the power sin is holding over us. He has the power to open any door in our lives—there's nowhere he cannot go.

Prayer for Morning

Jesus, you are the key of our salvation and you open the shackles that bind us. Come into my life today, especially to the rooms within that I don't know how to open to you. Key of David, bring me into freedom.

Ponder Today

How will Jesus approach me today? What doors of my life will he knock on, and how can I welcome him?

Prayer for Evening

Jesus, Emmanuel, your love opens new horizons for us, and you lead us into newness of life. Help me to step more deeply into your intimacy with the Father. Key of David, let me rest in you.

To listen to "O Come, O Come, Emmanuel," scan the QR code or visit

Saturday, December 7

FIRST WEEK OF ADVENT

Bid all our sad divisions cease and be yourself our King of Peace.

We know division all too well—we are very good at drawing lines between "them" and "us." We're so good at division that we live with it subconsciously; we've built it into our cities and smartphones. Sometimes the divisions we create make possible violence and war; sometimes they make possible the stubborn ignorance of our neighbors living radically different lives than we do.

As much as we long for peace, it will always elude us if we try to establish it on merely human terms. There is only one source of enduring unity: our shared dignity as children of God—a dignity that Jesus himself entered into. If we can find each other in him, then we will know peace.

Prayer for Morning

Jesus, our brother, you came to share our humanity so we could share in your divinity. Open my heart to see that you are inviting everyone I encounter today into communion with you and our heavenly Father. King of Peace, bind our hearts as one.

Ponder Today

Where will I experience division today? How can I let Jesus help me overcome it?

Prayer for Evening

Jesus, our Savior, you came to bring peace. Heal the divisions that cause so much suffering in the world, and heal the division I experience in my own heart. King of nations, make us whole.

Sunday, December 8

SECOND WEEK OF ADVENT

Ave Maria, gratia plena, Dominus tecum.
Hail Mary, full of grace, the Lord is with you.

For all the dramatic movements in this music, the words to the hymn "Ave Maria" simply repeat the lines of the well-known Hail Mary prayer. The melody soars with a sense of longing that builds and recedes—it feels *full*, like breathing deeply in front of a grand landscape. It makes us want to linger, as if there is too much to relish here. If we can slow down enough to let this hymn echo within us, we can touch a bit of the fullness that marked Mary's life. God filled her with grace so that she would be ready to bear Jesus to the world, and wants to fill us with grace as well.

Prayer for Morning

Mary, you were practiced at receiving gifts from God. Help me follow your example: to let go of fear and create room where Jesus can dwell within me. Mother Mary, help me follow your receptive faithfulness.

Ponder Today

When will I encounter moments of fullness today—especially in the ordinary—and how can I lift my heart to God in response?

Prayer for Evening

Holy Mary, your life was built around prayer. You knew how to hear and respond to God's voice, how to find peace in his will for your life. Pray for me, that I may cultivate that same intimacy with God. Mother Mary, help me follow your steady faithfulness.

To listen to "Ave Maria," scan the QR code or visit https://www.

Monday, December 9

FEAST OF THE IMMACULATE CONCEPTION

Benedicta tu in mulieribus, et benedictus fructus ventris tui, Jesus.
Blessed are you among women and blessed is the fruit
of your womb, Jesus.

Ave Maria or Hail Mary is one of the most Catholic expressions we have. It was first uttered by the angel Gabriel when he greeted Mary to announce the news that she was to bear Jesus. But we take on his greeting ourselves and also "hail" her, laud her, and raise her up. She is one of us, but she has been elevated as Mother of God, an elevation that began the moment she was conceived in her own mother's womb. With today's feast, we celebrate this moment of God's abundant grace.

God gave Mary the capacity to accomplish what he asked of her, and he does the same for us. When we struggle, when we face darkness or uncertainty, God calls us to rely on him and is ever ready to give us what we need.

Prayer for Morning

Mary, you brought the Son of God into our broken world, humbly accepting this charge. Pray for me, that I might live the life God is calling me to. Blessed Mother, help me grow in faith, hope, and love.

Ponder Today

How can I rely on God today? What situation or relationship needs God's saving grace?

Prayer for Evening

Mary, God had a special role for you to play in the salvation of the world. Pray for me, that I may find in the circumstances of my life right now the role God is asking me to fill. Blessed Mother, help me to do the Father's will.

avemariapress.com/let-heaven-and-nature-sing-music.

Tuesday, December 10

SECOND WEEK OF ADVENT

The King shall come when morning dawns
and light triumphant breaks,
when beauty gilds the eastern hills and life to joy awakes.

John the Baptist speaks to us in this second week of Advent, calling us to prepare the way for Christ's coming. It's time to remove the obstacles within our hearts and in our life circumstances that stand in the way of Jesus coming to us. He is always reaching for us, ready to conquer whatever diminishes us. John urges us to receive Jesus as a king—to clear space for him right now so that Christ reigns at the center of our lives.

Our hymn for today invites us to stand with others watching for our king to come, people who know that "light triumphant breaks" upon us in the person of Jesus. By setting aside our egos and placing him at the center, "life to joy awakes."

Prayer for Morning

Lord of Light, you reveal to us the fullness of God's love, which is as beautiful and inevitable as the dawn. Break over me in the same way the sun gilds the landscape in these long winter mornings. Help me prepare for your coming so I can greet you with joy. Jesus our king, triumph in me today.

Ponder Today

How can I prepare a way and straighten a path for the Lord today?

Prayer for Evening

Lord of Light, your love and truth illuminate our lives. Prepare your way in my heart—build in me the desire to receive you so that my life reflects your light. Jesus our king, make straight my path.

To listen to "The King Shall Come When Morning Dawns," scan the QR

Wednesday, December 11

SECOND WEEK OF ADVENT

The King shall come when morning dawns,
and light and beauty brings;
"Hail, Christ the Lord!" Thy people pray,
come quickly, King of kings!

To proclaim that Christ is our king says something about him and about us. We wait for the coming of the King of kings as part of a community seeking to live in God's ways.

This song proclaims our confidence that the Lord will come and will triumph over our lives as the sun conquers the darkness of night. Our confident waiting makes us distinctive as a people: we know the folly of seeking fulfillment in the things of this world, and we long to find our fulfillment in Christ. Advent is a time for us to go about the work of preparing a way for the Lord to conquer us.

Prayer for Morning

Lord Jesus Christ, you came to establish your reign among us, a reign that brings us light and beauty. Transform my desires so that I can let go of the things that distract and impede your way in me. Christ our king, conquer my heart.

Ponder Today

In what ways—even if they are small—will God's kingdom break into my experience today?

Prayer for Evening

Lord Jesus Christ, you are always calling us to a deeper union with you. Grant me the courage and honesty to see how I settle for less. Help me to follow you to the Father's love. Christ our king, deepen my desire for you.

code or visit https://www.avemariapress.com/let-heaven-and-nature-sing-music.

Thursday, December 12

FEAST OF OUR LADY OF GUADALUPE

Desde el cielo, una hermosa mañana,
La Guadalupana, bajó al Tepeyac.
From heaven on a beautiful morning,
the Guadalupan Lady came down to Tepeyac.

In 1532, on Tepeyac Hill in northern Mexico, Our Lady of Guadalupe approached Juan Diego with flowers and music, symbols of heaven in his culture. She dressed like him and spoke to him in Nahuatl, his first language. Our Lady came to Juan Diego in the same way Jesus comes to us—by moving toward us first, seeking us out in our ordinary experience. This is what love is: stepping beyond oneself to encounter and embrace another.

For today's feast, we pray with a festive hymn that retells the story of Juan Diego and Our Lady. In the retelling, we remember that she also comes to us right where we are.

Prayer for Morning

Mary, our Mother, you came to invigorate faith in your Son here in the Americas. Give me courage and use me as your messenger.

Ponder Today

How can I follow Mary's model of encounter today by noticing a detail or preference from someone and taking an active interest in their story?

Prayer for Evening

Mother Mary, you protect and hold us under your mantle. Help me to trust in your care for me—that you are ready to receive me as I am and will bring my concerns and worries to your son. Our Lady of Guadalupe, pray for me.

To listen to "La Guadalupana (The Virgin of Guadalupe)" and

Friday, December 13

SECOND WEEK OF ADVENT

Dona nobis pacem, pacem. Dona nobis pacem.
Grant us peace, peace. Grant us peace.

This song carries us along with one simple phrase—"grant us peace," perhaps one of the most elemental prayers we hold in common. Because of this simplicity and the yearning flow of the melody, it's been used in many contexts—both sacred and secular. The cast of the hit television series M*A*S*H famously sang it to close out the show's 1978 Christmas episode. And many of those who gathered to commemorate the beginning of the end of the Berlin Wall in November 1989 joined in singing it.

Traditionally attributed to Mozart, no one really knows where this hymn came from. It has endured because it works—it gathers hearts and unites us in prayer. Singing in rounds, we join people from around the world and across centuries who also long for peace.

Prayer for Morning

God of Peace, you created each of us in your image, yet we damage that inherent dignity with war and conflict. So many suffer from the pain we inflict upon each other. God of Love, help me treat justly and with love all whom I meet this day.

Ponder Today

How can I learn more about those who suffer because of war, and how can I support them with prayer, advocacy, or material aid?

Prayer for Evening

God of Peace, your love unites all humanity. Stir peace within all hearts, and grant us this night a peaceful rest.

"Dona nobis pacem (Grant us peace)," scan the QR code or visit https://www. avemariapress.com/let-heaven-and-nature-sing-music.

Saturday, December 14

SECOND WEEK OF ADVENT

Dona nobis pacem.
Grant us peace.

Just before we receive Communion at Mass, we look upon the Lamb of God, held high for us at the altar, and we ask the Lamb, Christ our Lord, to grant us peace.

Together, by this prayer, we say aloud that we lack peace—that we need it, that something in us is restless and unwhole and broken. We say those words because we know that we've tried to find peace elsewhere and failed. And we can't fabricate peace for ourselves—we've tried that as well. We find peace only in the one who came to reveal God's love for us, who shows us this way of love, who gives us this love, and who is love itself—through him, with him, and in him. Only in Christ do we, and our broken world, find peace.

Prayer for Morning

Lord Jesus, you know the needs of every human heart. Guide me with your truth, so that in conforming my life to yours I may find peace and purpose. Lamb of God, show me your way; teach me to live in your peace.

Ponder Today

What consistently disturbs my peace, and how can I turn it over to God?

Prayer for Evening

Lord Jesus, you are our only source of peace. Help me let go of the things I cling to in search of this peace. Lamb of God, have mercy on me.

To listen to "Dona nobis pacem (Grant us peace)" and "Come, Thou

Sunday, December 15

THIRD WEEK OF ADVENT

Come, thou long expected Jesus, born to set thy people free;
from our fears and sins release us, let us find our rest in thee.

In 1744, Charles Wesley was preaching the Gospel throughout England. Between his engagements, he passed children in great need—orphans doing what they had to do to survive on the streets or in menial labor. It's not hard to picture how they looked at Charles as he exited churches full of well-dressed Christians. The awkward disharmony of preaching the Good News and witnessing such poverty all around him sparked a longing in Charles to see this upside-down world overturned, and he was inspired to write the hymn we pray with today, "Come, Thou Long-Expected Jesus."

Born thy people to deliver, born a child and yet a King, we sing in the second verse. In the hungry eyes looking at him, Charles saw the face of Christ, who was also born into a poor family seeking shelter—a child who was also a king. We join him to pray for our long-expected Lord to come to *reign in us forever, now thy gracious kingdom bring*.

Prayer for Morning

Jesus, you are our strength and consolation, the joy of every longing heart. Help me to recognize you in your coming to me today, especially as you are present with those who suffer. Holy One, deliver me from evil.

Ponder Today

What conflict and disharmony do I notice in my corner of the world?

Prayer for Evening

Jesus, you are the hope of all the earth and the desire of every nation. Only you can release me from fear and sin. Meet me in my longing for you and free me. Holy One, I find my rest in you.

Long Expected Jesus," scan the QR code or visit *https://www.avemariapress.com/let-heaven-and-nature-sing-music.*

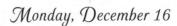

Monday, December 16

THIRD WEEK OF ADVENT

Born thy people to deliver, born a child and yet a King,
born to reign in us forever, now thy gracious kingdom bring.

For an Advent song, there is a startling lack of a manger scene or Nativity story—no angels or shepherds in this song we continue praying with today. This is a hymn about longing for Christ to come again in justice and glory, and that names us part of a people who have long awaited this Savior.

We experience injustice everywhere, in our own relationships and among the nations. Yet we wait for Christ to come and make all things—not just us—right and whole. This is a waiting that builds our hope, deepens our resolve, and shores up the resilience we need to work for the kingdom of God. The watchful longing we practice throughout Advent allows us to find joy and light where the world sees only darkness because we know the Lord is near.

Prayer for Morning

God our Creator, you made me with a heart to search and know you, and you do not refuse to answer my longing for you. Grow my desire for the gifts you have to give me. God of hope, send your Son into my life.

Ponder Today

What is competing with my desire for the Lord today?

Prayer for Evening

God our Creator, you made me for joy. Incline my heart toward your grace so that I can look for your coming to me with confidence and hope. God of hope, center me in your love.

To listen to "Come, Thou Long Expected Jesus," scan the QR code or

Tuesday, December 17

THIRD WEEK OF ADVENT

By thine own eternal spirit rule in all our hearts alone;
by thine all sufficient merit, raise us to thy glorious throne.

The peaks and valleys of the melody we've been praying with this week mirror the movements in the prayerful words. The music feels like ascending and descending flights of steps. We pray for a long-expected gracious king to bring us freedom and rest. And we pray for the reign of this Savior to lift us up: "By thine own eternal spirit rule in all our hearts alone . . . raise us to thy glorious throne."

This is why God came among us as one of us: to let us share in the divine life of the Trinity. This transformation can only happen when we let Christ "rule in our hearts." Entrusting ourselves to a savior means shaping our lives according to his life. This obedience looks confining to the world, but we know it leads us to freedom because it makes us into the people we were created to be: God's own children, destined for heaven.

Prayer for Morning

Holy Spirit, you are the breath of the Creator within us, bringing us life. Breathe in me and through me; sustain me in your communion with the Father and the Son. Spirit of glory, raise me up.

Ponder Today

What part of my daily experience do I keep to myself, and how can I invite Jesus to rule there?

Prayer for Evening

Holy Spirit, restore in me the image of our Creator. Help me to conform my life to Jesus so I can share more fully in his divine life. Spirit of glory, lead me to freedom.

visit https://www.avemariapress.com/let-heaven-and-nature-sing-music.

✦

Wednesday, December 18

THIRD WEEK OF ADVENT

O come, divine Messiah; the world in silence waits the day
when hope shall sing its triumph and sadness flee away.

What does it sound like for hope to "sing its triumph"? How is the world
waiting in silence? And what does it mean that both images come alive for
us in music that is filling our ears and hearts?

Our experience of the world is not very quiet. Even when we strip
away the noises we layer over our lives, we are surrounded by constant
sounds vying for our attention. But the kind of silence we're singing about
is more like stillness. There is a space in our center that is quiet stillness if
we can peel back the layers of distraction to make room for it. Advent is
a good time to practice stepping into that space, even when our world is
noisy, because that is where we meet our divine Messiah.

Prayer for Morning

Divine Messiah, you came to earth to dispel the night with the dawn of
grace. Help me empty myself to make room for you, and let your light
and peace sing their triumph in my heart. Jesus, I wait for you in stillness.

Ponder Today

In the midst of all this day will bring, when can I step into stillness?

Prayer for Evening

Divine Messiah, you are the fulfillment of my longing, but I too easily fill
this desire with lesser goods. Help me to set aside the things that crowd
out your silent, waiting presence, for you long for me too. Jesus, show me
your face.

To listen to "O Come, Divine Messiah," scan the QR code or visit

Thursday, December 19

THIRD WEEK OF ADVENT

O Christ, whom nations sigh for, whom priest
and prophet long foretold,
come, break the captive's fetters, redeem the long-lost fold.

Our Advent waiting should change the way we see. Our preparation should teach us how to welcome Christ into our lives and how to recognize the ways Christ is already acting in our daily experience. Advent is an apprenticeship into life in the kingdom of God. We are practicing new ways to recognize and participate in this reign that is already with us.

This apprenticeship means seeing the world from Christ's point of view—to see what God desires for us. This vision faces continual challenges from the world and from our own self-centeredness. Over and over, we fall short of God's dreams for us. So we pray for hope and courage and sing with this hymn for redemption in Christ.

Prayer for Morning

Creator, you created me for fullness of life in union with you through your Son. Grant me perseverance to keep striving for life with you and an open heart to recognize all the ways you share your love with me. God of Love, bring me closer to you today.

Ponder Today

What does my life look like through God's eyes? What are his desires for me?

Prayer for Evening

Creator, you continue to remake the world, moment by moment, as you establish your kingdom here on earth. Help me see your creative work in my life and respond with gratitude. God of Love, may your kingdom come.

https://www.avemariapress.com/let-heaven-and-nature-sing-music.

Friday, December 20

THIRD WEEK OF ADVENT

You come in peace and meekness and lowly will your cradle be;
all clothed in human weakness shall we your Godhead see.

Most Nativity scenes enshrine the Holy Family in light and peaceful wonder. The soft glow emanating from the manger where the baby Jesus lay tells us of the consolation of God's nearness, but the night of Jesus's birth must have felt out of control for Mary. It's not hard to imagine Mary's exhaustion and Joseph's worries. Jesus almost certainly cried.

This hymn reminds us that Christ still comes "clothed in human weakness" and that we can see his divinity in poverty—our own and our world's. With the eyes of faith, we can find Jesus reaching for us in all those who are impoverished and in our own weakness.

Prayer for Morning

Jesus, our Savior, you reveal the Father's tender mercy and compassion. When I feel out of control or powerless, you are by my side. Help me turn to you when I am weak, to rely on your love as the foundation of my life. Jesus, my brother, you are my strength.

Ponder Today

Where will I encounter vulnerability today, and how will I find Jesus there?

Prayer for Evening

Jesus, our Savior, you came into the most broken parts of our humanity to raise us to the splendor of divine life. Increase my faith so that I look to you and cling to you when that divine life feels far away. Jesus, my brother, hold me close.

To listen to "O Come, Divine Messiah," scan the QR code or visit

Saturday, December 21

THIRD WEEK OF ADVENT

Dear Savior, haste! Come, come to earth.
Dispel the night and show your face,
and bid us hail the dawn of grace.

Jesus has already come to earth—so what are we praying for so urgently? Advent is a time to cultivate the virtue of patience. In becoming aware of our need for a savior, we develop an urgent longing to encounter him soon—now. The gap between our longing and his coming is a place where we can sit firmly to wait for him to show his face.

This kind of waiting is the practice of Christian hope. Unless Jesus's second coming arrives before then, we know the world will not be drastically different on December 25. But we can be different. Indeed, we are *supposed* to be different because of our watching and waiting.

Prayer for Morning

Jesus, you came to earth two thousand years ago, and you will return one day to transform this world with your glory. Until then, come to the patch of earth I will tread today and be my companion. Dear Savior, I wait for you.

Ponder Today

When will I encounter impatience today, and how can I translate that into prayer?

Prayer for Evening

Jesus, as we prepare to welcome you anew into our lives with our Christmas feast, you reveal to us all the ways you are already acting in our experience to bring us life. Draw me closer to the Father with you. Dear Savior, show me your life-giving ways.

https://www.avemariapress.com/let-heaven-and-nature-sing-music.

Sunday, December 22

FOURTH WEEK OF ADVENT

Creator of the stars of night, your people's everlasting light,
O Christ, Redeemer of us all, we pray you, hear us when we call.

In this last week of Advent, in the final days before our Christmas feast, we take on the disposition of expectant stillness. In today's gospel reading, we join Mary as she visits her cousin Elizabeth—both of them aware of a great mystery unfolding in their bodies, one that will change the course of history but remains hidden.

This ancient hymn we pray with today and tomorrow captures a paradox we embrace every Advent: God is presented as Creator of the stars of night, which are grand, vast, distant, and cold; at the same time, God came to us not as a powerful king but in that tender moment when parents hold their infant for the first time. The fact that both of these images of God are true pulls us into wonder and humility.

Prayer for Morning

Almighty God, you are our creator and the one who fashioned the churning galaxies. Despite your power and majesty, help me to believe that you are close to me. Come near to me and increase my capacity to perceive you present and growing within me. Creator, make me new.

Ponder Today

When will I be able to practice wonder and humility today?

Prayer for Evening

Almighty God, you are a mystery unfolding in each of our lives. Help me to remember that each act of love—even the seemingly insignificant—is a participation in your life. Creator, help me see your nearness.

To listen to "Creator of the Stars of Night," scan the QR code or visit

Monday, December 23

FOURTH WEEK OF ADVENT

When earth drew on to darkest night, you came,
but not in splendor bright,
not as a king, but the child of Mary, virgin mother mild.

Here, on the other side of the winter solstice, is a good time to appreciate light as a precious commodity and acknowledge how much we depend on it. As much as we depend on the natural light of the sun, we need the light of God's love even more. When we turn away from the Light of the World, we get lost, we stumble, and we lose hope.

Sometimes this means we fall into the darkness of sin, but even more often, we live in a kind of gray dusk where everything looks the same. It can be hard to believe that there's something transcendent behind the dullness of the ordinary, where little changes about our lives. Without a sense of wonder, our daily lives can seem burdensome.

Jesus came to be with us, which means these burdens are places where he is ready to share his everlasting life and light with us.

Prayer for Morning

Light of the World, you came to bring us divine life, becoming human in all things. Help me welcome your love, which brings warmth and color, so I can see clearly and live with boldness. Jesus, bring me your light.

Ponder Today

How can I invite Jesus to be with me in the insignificant parts of my day?

Prayer for Evening

Light of the World, we walk in darkness when we try to live without you. Draw me again to your everlasting light, where I find eternal purpose. Jesus, bring me your love.

https://www.avemariapress.com/let-heaven-and-nature-sing-music.

Tuesday, December 24

CHRISTMAS EVE

Silent night! Holy night! All is calm, all is bright
'round yon virgin mother and child! Holy infant, so tender and mild,
sleep in heavenly peace.

Tonight marks the end of our Advent preparation as we stand on the threshold of our Christmas feast and look back at how our hearts have been formed by the music and prayer we've engaged in together. The songs we've been praying with have created a disposition within us—something that begins as a feeling but is more like a posture. The music has been giving us shoes to stand in before God and has shaped the silence of our prayer.

This holy night may be full of the sounds of preparation and conversation and family and celebration but is also full of solemn, quiet wonder. Tonight, we bow before the gift of God-with-us, who not only waits to meet us in prayer but also comes to stand in *our* shoes.

Prayer for Morning

Christ our Savior, as I listen for your voice speaking in my life, help me to hear your heart beating with mine, for you are closer than I can imagine. Lord Jesus, make me calm and bright.

Ponder Today

How can I step into silence today—even just a few minutes—to anchor my entry into this feast?

Prayer for Evening

Christ our Savior, you are the Son of God and love's pure light. Help me see your glory streaming toward us. Lord Jesus, bring me your heavenly peace.

To listen to "Silent Night" and "Joy to the World," scan the QR code

Wednesday, December 25

CHRISTMAS DAY

Joy to the world, the Lord is come! Let earth receive her King!
Let every heart prepare him room, and heav'n and nature sing,
and heav'n and nature sing, and heav'n, and heav'n and nature sing.

This song is structured joy. The second half of each verse is simply the same phrase stacked on top of itself over and over until it tumbles over. It's hard to sing without feeling some of that momentum thrumming in your chest.

"Let every heart prepare him room," we sing. Now is the time to receive our King. Our feast is marked by great joy because of the gift we've been given. Although we've been working to increase our capacity to receive him, he still comes to us undeservedly and gratuitously. Today we find God's grace crashing over us beyond what we've been preparing for, beyond even what we can grasp!

Prayer for Morning

Jesus, our Lord, you bring heaven and nature together, and we join the chorus of creation today to praise you. I trust your love to conquer my brokenness and imperfection. Jesus, my King, thank you for your deep and abiding love.

Ponder Today

What glimpses of joy—small or large—can I delight in today?

Prayer for Evening

Jesus, our Lord, you were present at creation and rule the universe—and yet you humbled yourself to join our wounded world. I offer you gratitude and praise as I contemplate the magnitude of this gift. Jesus, my King, may your love rule over me.

or visit https://www.avemariapress.com/let-heaven-and-nature-sing-music.

Thursday, December 26

CHRISTMAS WEEKDAY

Joy to the earth, the Savior reigns! Let men their songs employ,
while fields and floods, rocks, hills, and plains
repeat the sounding joy.

"Joy to the earth, the Savior reigns!" But does he? What signs do we have of his kingdom? If we celebrate the coming of our Savior at Christmas, why doesn't today look different from last Thursday?

As our Advent longing becomes Christmas joy, we continue tending the interior space where friendship with Jesus takes root. This is the first place we encounter God's kingdom and where Jesus's life takes shape in us. This doesn't mean that changing the world stage is beyond our abilities, only that it comes as a fruit of the life of Christ within us. This divine life overflows in our service and advocacy for justice and peace, as it did for St. Stephen whose feast marks this day. But our task for today is to repeat the joy sounding through creation at the coming of our Savior.

Prayer for Morning

Mighty One, you sent your Son as our Savior. I join with all of your people as we use both music and attentive stillness to sing your praise. God of creation, let your joy resound in me.

Ponder Today

How can I let the Savior reign in me today? How might that lead me to joy?

Prayer for Evening

Mighty One, your Son comes to draw all of creation to you. Give me ears to hear the sounding joy of this eternal destiny. God of creation, let me repeat for others your self-giving love.

To listen to "Joy to the World" and "Hark the Herald Angels Sing,"

Friday, December 27

CHRISTMAS WEEKDAY

Hark! the herald angels sing, "Glory to the newborn King:
peace on earth, and mercy mild, God and sinners reconciled!"

Here in the octave of Christmas, we join the angels who herald the dawn of peace and mercy with the coming of Jesus—the one who has created a new way for us, the one in whom "God and sinners are reconciled."

We continue to turn away from God in our selfishness and greed; we are fallen people, and no matter how good our intentions are, we can't seem to stay out of trouble. Yet God our Father refuses to let us break the relationship—he comes to us to draw us to him *through* that self-centered folly. And he comes to us in the most intimate way possible: by entering our human condition and bearing our wounds. Still, we sin; still, we suffer, but we are not condemned to the prison of our own guilt and shame. We are made for more, and God has moved heaven and earth to make sure we get there.

Prayer for Morning

Saving God, you offer me the fullness of your own divine life—your very self—in your Son. He comes to be born in me today, even now in this moment. Help me set aside whatever holds me back from fully embracing your love for me. Loving Father, be here with me.

Ponder Today

How can I herald God's loving care for someone in my life today?

Prayer for Evening

Saving God, there is nothing I can do to separate myself from you. Grant me patient confidence in your care for me so that even my twisted path can lead me back to you. Loving Father, let me join the triumph of your love.

scan the QR code or visit https://www.avemariapress.com/let-heaven-and-nature-sing-music.

Saturday, December 28

CHRISTMAS WEEKDAY

Light and life to all he brings, risen with healing in his wings.
Mild he lays his glory by, born that we no more may die,
born to raise us from the earth, born to give us second birth.

Christ comes to us enfleshed in the circumstances of our daily lives, just as God came in the infant Jesus to Mary and Joseph. They were faithful people who worshiped in synagogues and the Temple, but the bulk of their role in bearing and raising God's Son took place in the context of washing clothes and fixing wobbly tables and negotiating the opinions of in-laws and neighbors. This means that Jesus also comes to us in the context of our own ordinary, daily routines and challenges.

Yes, Jesus came to "raise us from the earth" and to "give us second birth" in communion with the Triune God. With our Christmas feast, we celebrate the mystery that we don't have to go searching for this new life—he comes to us.

Prayer for Morning

Sun of Righteousness, splendor of the Father, you bring me light and life. Help me to recognize your glory in the parts of my life that feel most dreary and dull. Prince of Peace, raise me to new life in you.

Ponder Today

In what area of my life do I most desire to experience new life?

Prayer for Evening

Sun of Righteousness, in you I need not fear death and nothingness—I don't even have to fear my own brokenness and cycles of sin. Prince of Peace, make me whole in you.

To listen to "Hark the Herald Angels Sing" and "What Child Is This?,"

Sunday, December 29

FEAST OF THE HOLY FAMILY

What Child is this, who, laid to rest, on Mary's lap is sleeping?
Whom angels greet with anthems sweet,
while shepherds watch are keeping?

Our hymn for today and tomorrow, "What Child Is This," reminds us that Christ, our King, comes to us as a child sleeping on Mary's lap. Imagine her in a quiet moment of rest, gazing upon him as an infant. With her, we can see his slow breathing, his eyes twitching below the lids, and his tiny mouth drawing whispers of breath. As she adjusts her legs, picture the way his back arches into a spontaneous stretch before he settles back into her familiar warmth.

Imagine Joseph watching the two of them, wondering what kind of mystery the three of them have entered, and even more enthralled by the way a new kind of love has taken shape before him. Where will this love lead the new family?

Prayer for Morning

Mary, Mother of God, you hold me with the same tender care with which you held Jesus. As my mother in faith, help me to grow in hope and love through your Son. Blessed Mary, pray for me today.

Ponder Today

In what ways might my family be leading me to more clearly see and rely on God's love?

Prayer for Evening

Joseph, Guardian of Mary and Jesus, you wondered at the mystery of love as it grew before you in family life. Help me to also ponder with reverent gratitude the ways love takes shape in my life. Blessed Joseph, pray for me.

scan the QR code or visit https://www.avemariapress.com/let-heaven-and-nature-sing-music.

Monday, December 30

CHRISTMAS WEEKDAY

Why lies He in such mean estate, where ox and ass are feeding?
Good Christian, fear: for sinners here the silent Word is pleading.

We know Jesus as the Word—God's self-communication to us. Jesus speaks to us through his words and actions as they are recorded in the gospels and in the ongoing friendship through which he is present to our everyday living. In our Christmas feast, however, we recall his infancy, when he was unable to say or do anything. At his coming—the moment when heaven and earth met—the only thing the Son of God was able to communicate was his need and dependence and vulnerability, and the only people he could communicate with were two parents far from home.

What a strange thing for God to say to us with his Word! The One who created us has confined himself to the smallest, quietest part of our experience, where he fully inhabits it. Nothing we experience is foreign to him—he is the Word who pleads for us through his silence.

Prayer for Morning

Jesus, Word of the Father, you reveal that God is love. Conform my heart to yours that I may enter your life by giving my own away. Word of Love, speak to me today.

Ponder Today

What word can I silently share with others through my actions today?

Prayer for Evening

Jesus, Word of the Father, you came to bring us salvation. Spur my heart with urgent praise that I may enthrone you there as my King. Word of Love, help me hear your voice.

To listen to "What Child Is This" and "There Is No Rose of Such

Tuesday, December 31

CHRISTMAS WEEKDAY

The angels sang the shepherds to: *gloria in excelsis Deo:*
gaudeamus [Glory to God in the highest: let us rejoice].
Now leave we all this worldly mirth and follow we this joyful birth;
transeamus [let us pass over].

It happened in the Garden of Eden, and it happens in every one of us—sin spoils our relationship with God. But our brokenness is not our destiny. This hope is why, in the words of our hymn for today, "leave we all this worldly mirth and follow we this joyful birth."

The music here resonates as boldly as the words. Spend a few moments listening to the Notre Dame Folk Choir rendition of this hymn, "Rosa Mystica" (at the link below), and note the dynamics with which we sing *transeamus*. Three different voices intone it, each at a lower note that stretches upward until the fourth voice enters above them all. It's a nice portrayal of how we each long for union with God, stretching toward heaven until the Word descends to join us and we pass over together.

Prayer for Morning

Triune God, the mystery of your love took shape in our humanity in the baby Jesus. Help me follow him into union with you. I sing with the angels and shepherds: glory to God in the highest!

Ponder Today

What "worldly mirth" am I being called to leave behind for a greater joy?

Prayer for Evening

Triune God, three persons in one who create, redeem, and sanctify me, help me to follow the way of our Savior—fill me with your Spirit, and create me anew. Loving God, increase my joy and awe at the magnitude of your love.

Virtue," scan the QR code or visit https://www.avemariapress.com/let-heaven-and-nature-sing-music.

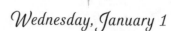

Wednesday, January 1

SOLEMNITY OF MARY, MOTHER OF GOD

There is no rose of such virtue as is the rose that bare Jesu;
alleluia.
For in this rose contained was heaven and earth in little space;
res miranda [a thing to be wondered at].

This hymn we pray with again today ponders Mary as a rose who contains heaven and earth in the person of Jesus. A thing to be wondered at, indeed, that the One who was present at creation consented to be carried by her. How can this be? Think of a dewdrop in the folds of a rose—a close examination reveals the whole world refracted within the liquid sphere.

We, too, are called to such virtue: to imitate Mary as a rose catching the dewfall of the Holy Spirit. Jesus is ready to be carried by us as well, to take on life within us as we bear him to people in darkness waiting to see God's face.

Prayer for Morning

Holy Mary, Mother of God, your faithfulness allowed us to see God's face in Jesus, your Son. Pray for me, that I may grow in faith and so share him with others in need. Mary, our mother, help me to carry Jesus today.

Ponder Today

What opportunity might I seize today to cultivate virtue?

Prayer for Evening

Holy Mary, Mother of God, Jesus contained himself within the little space of your womb so that God could contain us in his love. Help me create space for your Son to also dwell in me. Mary, our mother, lead me with your prayerfulness.

To listen to "There Is No Rose of Such Virtue" and "O Come, All Ye

Thursday, January 2

CHRISTMAS WEEKDAY

Yea, Lord, we greet thee, born this happy morning;
Jesus, to Thee be all glory giv'n!
Word of the Father, now in flesh appearing!

This spirited hymn begs to be belted out. The world marches on to New Year's resolutions, but we don't give up our Christmas feasting so easily. We stand ready to greet the Lord this happy morning, joyful and triumphant in our acknowledgment of this great gift.

The key to keeping up our Christmas spirit is to stay grounded in our awareness of our need for a savior. Anyone with a conscience should not have to reflect very long to conclude that though we bear God's image, we are incomplete and broken. But we've been given glad tidings of the "Word of the Father, now in flesh appearing"—the One who reveals that nothing can stand in the way of God's desire for communion with us. It is a day to be joyful and triumphant indeed.

Prayer for Morning

Jesus my brother, I celebrate your coming among us—a surprising and undeserved gift that began in Bethlehem and continues to this day. Help me sustain my joy and gratitude for the gift of your presence with me in this moment, here and now. Christ, my Lord, let me sing in exultation.

Ponder Today

How might I continue my Christmas festivity today?

Prayer for Evening

Jesus my brother, there is nowhere I can go and nothing I can do to lessen your love for me. You reign over heaven and earth—reign in me as well. Christ, my Lord, I adore you.

Faithful," scan the QR code or visit https://www.avemariapress.com/let-heaven-and-nature-sing-music.

Friday, January 3

CHRISTMAS WEEKDAY

O come, all ye faithful, joyful and triumphant,
O come ye, O come ye to Bethlehem!
Come, and behold him, born the King of angels!

We began Advent more than a month ago by praying with "O Come, O Come, Emmanuel." Here in our Christmas celebration, we continue to sing "O Come"—but this time as a jubilant invitation to all the faithful to come adore our newborn King and behold our very God who has committed himself to us in an unexpected and strange way.

We are pursued by a God of surprises, who is unpredictable in his methods but constant in his love. Having encountered the wonderful ways he comes into the most secret corners of our experience, we can't help but proclaim this good news: come and behold the King of angels!

Prayer for Morning

Lord Jesus, King of angels, wealthy wise men and poor shepherds alike came to give you homage at your birth. I join them and all your people who greet you this happy morning to give you glory. Emmanuel, I want to behold you today.

Ponder Today

Where has God hidden himself in the circumstances of my life?

Prayer for Evening

Lord Jesus, King of angels, you are the image of the invisible God born in a stable among the livestock. Come into the parts of my life that feel unprepared, ordinary, and dark and save me from thinking you want only the best of me. Emmanuel, I present my whole self to you.

To listen to "O Come, All Ye Faithful," scan the QR code or visit

Saturday, January 4

CHRISTMAS WEEKDAY

Sing, choirs of angels; sing in exultation;
sing, all ye citizens of heav'n above!
Glory to God, all glory in the highest!
O come, let us adore him, Christ, the Lord!

When we praise God, our lives are rightly ordered. Giving God thanks, joined together with all the angels and saints, means acknowledging ourselves as creatures and God as Creator. But we cannot rightly adore the Lord if we elevate our own egos or are swallowed up by our woundedness. Raising our voices in praise with the holy ones in heaven magnifies them, so let us join all the faithful and sing with full hearts: "Glory to God, all glory in the highest!"

Prayer for Morning

Almighty Creator, you made me for relationship with you and placed a desire for this communion deep in my heart. Send me your grace so I may seek and know you—and praise you more fully. Our Father, restore me.

Ponder Today

How can I adore Jesus today—either inside a church building or in the people who are part of my life?

Prayer for Evening

Almighty Creator, your Son seeks to make all people one human family redeemed by your love. Be with my loved ones near and far, especially those who have died, and bring all of us into your divine life, where we will experience the fullness of communion together in you. Our Father, draw us together in you.

https://www.avemariapress.com/let-heaven-and-nature-sing-music.

January 5

EPIPHANY SUNDAY

> We three kings of Orient are; bearing gifts we traverse afar,
> field and fountain, moor and mountain, following yonder star.

We can imagine that the Magi of Matthew's gospel were truth-seekers. They studied the heavens because they were curious about the world and our place in it. Their study led them to follow a strange sign in the sky, a phenomenon that they didn't fully understand that led them beyond the familiar. Instead of dismissing it because it was inconvenient, they pursued it, yearning to know more.

These wise men seem to know only that this star they followed was pointing to a new king. They weren't seeking him in order to curry favor or develop an alliance—they just wanted to understand and establish themselves in right relationship to him. They came prepared to honor this king and probably couldn't have imagined that he was a newborn living in lowly surroundings, and yet they followed where Truth seemed to lead.

Prayer for Morning

God of Truth, all of creation bears your fingerprints. Deepen my curiosity to perceive you in new ways, and grant me the courage to follow where you are leading. Mighty One, I seek you today.

Ponder Today

What inconvenient signs might be leading you to a deeper truth about your life?

Prayer for Evening

God of Truth, help me rest in you who are the deepest truth of my life. Mighty One, attune my heart to yours.

To listen to "We Three Kings of Orient Are," scan the QR code or visit

Monday, January 6

Christmas Weekday

O star of wonder, star of light, star with royal beauty bright,
westward leading, still proceeding, guide us to thy perfect light.

The Magi are famous for the gifts they brought—gold, frankincense, and myrrh—which communicated their understanding of the power this new king would bear. Their gold was a tribute to his royalty and an invitation for him to reign even from his home in Bethlehem. The fragrance of frankincense was associated with worship—they wanted to be part of a people who recognized the divine life of this king. With their myrrh—a burial perfume—they acknowledge a king who has come to share everything with his people, even their death.

The most impressive thing about these gifts is the preparation they involved—the kings anticipated whom they would find and were ready to recognize his significance with offerings that honored the lordship of Jesus.

Prayer for Morning

Jesus, Lord of heaven and earth, help me work toward establishing your kingdom today—both within myself and in my community. Jesus, our King, help me to follow your way.

Ponder Today

How can I make a gift of my life to God today in response to the mystery of his reign in me?

Prayer for Evening

Jesus, Lord of heaven and earth, you share in every aspect of my humanity—even death—as a way to conquer everything that might stand in the way of God's love for me. Deepen my faith in your love for me. Jesus, my King, reign in my heart.

https://www.avemariapress.com/let-heaven-and-nature-sing-music.

Tuesday, January 7

CHRISTMAS WEEKDAY

The first Noel the angel did say
was to certain poor shepherds in fields as they lay,
in fields where they lay keeping their sheep,
on a cold winter's night that was so deep.

The first half of our hymn for today and tomorrow draws us to the shepherds we know from our Nativity scenes. No one considered these outsiders important—they were nomads, out of the loop of the village news. They smelled. Yet these were the first people to receive the good news of the newborn king. Why?

Of the people within a one-mile radius of Jesus's birth, these shepherds were the poorest and most marginalized—they needed the good news he came to proclaim. From the moment of his arrival, even as an infant, Jesus is already accomplishing his mission. He comes to share this good news with us and to involve us in sharing it with others.

Prayer for Morning

Jesus, our newborn King, draw near to me now, and lead me to others who need this good news today. Jesus, my star, guide me in your way today.

Ponder Today

Who are the outsiders in my community, and how can I share good news with them?

Prayer for Evening

Jesus, our newborn King, grant me peace in my own seeking and use me as a herald of your love. Jesus, my star, lead me to deeper faith, hope, and love.

To listen to "The First Noel," scan the QR code or visit https://www.

Wednesday, January 8

CHRISTMAS WEEKDAY

Noel, Noel, Noel, Noel
born is the King of Israel.

The word "Noel" has its roots in the Latin *natalis*, for "birth." In French, it came to refer to Christmas, connotations that appear in English with our *Nativity* scenes. It is a strange word to repeat so often in this hymn, but maybe there is something significant in this simple refrain.

We sing of the "first" Noel with Jesus's birth, but his coming to us is not an event fixed in only one time and place. His birth was the definitive movement of God's arrival to our humanity, a movement that continues today. Here and now, in your prayer this morning, Jesus is coming to you, inviting you to receive him in the particularities of your experience today. As we repeat "Noel" with this song, let us use it as a longing invitation for Jesus to be born within us anew.

Prayer for Morning

Merciful Father, you reach for me in your Son, who comes to share life with me. With your grace, help me receive the new life Christ brings and find in him the answer to my longing. God of Love, draw me to you.

Ponder Today

What part of my life most needs to receive Jesus's healing and life-giving presence today?

Prayer for Evening

Merciful Father, you send your life-giving Spirit to renew me and guide my heart. Enlighten and strengthen me to do your will and live in your peace. God of Love, dwell in me.

avemariapress.com/let-heaven-and-nature-sing-music.

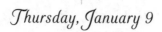

Thursday, January 9

CHRISTMAS WEEKDAY

Fall on your knees! O hear the angel voices!
O night divine, O night when Christ was born!
O night, O holy night, O night divine!

Ask the music director at your parish about "O Holy Night" and they'll tell you that it takes a lot of guts to lead a congregation through it—the wide vocal range makes it notoriously difficult. Yet, in the right hands, this music swells and soars and takes our longing hearts with it.

It's a good tune to convey the thrill of hope and rejoicing we feel at the undeserved and total gift of self by which God comes to us in Jesus. We are unable to escape our sin and error, as the hymn describes, but we have a way to the Father through Jesus. Christ was born to be our Savior who knows our need and is no stranger to our weakness.

Prayer for Morning

Dear Savior, your birth among us broke a new and glorious morning upon our humanity. Shine the warm rays of your light into my life this day. Jesus, friend, I come alive in you.

Ponder Today

When do I lose sight of my worth—and how can I invite Jesus into those experiences?

Prayer for Evening

Dear Savior, as this Christmas season draws to an end, I stand by your cradle with glowing heart. Despite a weary world, I continue to rejoice. In you, I sense the depth of God's love for me—help me make this love the most important reality in my life. Jesus, help me find my worth in you.

To listen to "O Holy Night," scan the QR code or visit https://www.

Friday, January 10

CHRISTMAS WEEKDAY

Chains shall He break, for the slave is our brother,
and in His name all oppression shall cease.
Sweet hymns of joy in grateful chorus raise we;
let all within us praise His holy name.

"O Holy Night" has its origins in France in 1843 and was adapted to English in 1855. It became a popular hymn in the northern US states because the third verse resonated with abolitionists: "Chains shall he break, for the slave is our brother, and in his name all oppression shall cease."

The abolitionists were right: we are all brothers and sisters joined together in Christ. But the consequences of his coming don't stop with that fact: Jesus continues to enter our experience and act in our relationships. If God is love, and Jesus is God's love in the full embrace of our humanity, then we participate in that love whenever we offer ourselves in self-gift to others. When we imitate Christ, we allow him to love *through* us.

Prayer for Morning

Christ the Lord, your love binds me to all other people. Perfect my love with unselfishness, patience, and generosity so I may make a more complete gift of myself to the people in my life. Dear Jesus, refine my heart.

Ponder Today

How can I call upon Jesus to deepen my love for someone today?

Prayer for Evening

Christ the Lord, your coming inaugurated God's reign here. Let me participate in your kingdom more fully so I can join your people in raising a chorus of grateful joy. Dear Jesus, let all within me praise you.

avemariapress.com/let-heaven-and-nature-sing-music.

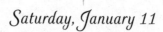

Saturday, January 11

CHRISTMAS WEEKDAY

Go tell it on the mountain, over the hills, and ev'rywhere;
go, tell it on the mountain that Jesus Christ is born.

Our hymn for today and tomorrow hails from the tradition of African American spiritual music. Originating among people who were enslaved, its authorship is uncertain, but it was passed along orally until it was published in 1907 by John Wesley Work Jr., a Black teacher and musician from Nashville. The people whose voices created this song faced some of the worst of our humanity, yet music helped them proclaim their faith.

This song does not plead or suggest that we should share the news of the birth of Jesus Christ—it commands us to go tell it from the highest place we can find. His holy birth needs to be known by all—not just believers, not just people in our circle, not just children, and not just those who are suffering, but everyone.

Prayer for Morning

Holy One, you were born into poverty in the cold, dark night, and all things came to be through you and continue to have life because of you. Grant me the grace to conform myself to you so that others may see you and call you Lord. Jesus, help me proclaim your kingdom.

Ponder Today

What difference does Jesus's birth make in my life?

Prayer for Evening

Holy One, you are the light who has come to enlighten everyone. Illuminate the darkness of this world and the shadowy corners of my life with your love, that I may testify to your light. Lord Jesus, shine in me.

To listen to "Go Tell It on the Mountain," scan the QR code or visit

Sunday, January 12

THE FEAST OF THE BAPTISM OF THE LORD

Down in a lowly manger the humble Christ was born,
and God sent us salvation that blessed Christmas morn.
Go tell it on the mountain, over the hills, and ev'rywhere.

What will we bring with us from this Advent and Christmas season into 2025? One of the gifts of this season is that it reminds us of the centrality of joy—a disposition that has consistently colored the music we've prayed with over the past weeks. Joy certainly drives this song, but even the hymns that express our longing and watching and waiting for a savior point us toward the expectant joy of God's people.

Joy is the mark of a Christian by virtue of our Baptism, which patterns our existence on Jesus's life, death, and resurrection. The coming of our Savior, and the divine life he shares with us, makes us God's own beloved children and offers us unending hope. What a wonderous gift that deserves to be shouted and shared over the hills and everywhere!

Prayer for Morning

Jesus, our beginning and end, through our baptism, you open to us the mystery of new life. Help me empty myself in love as you did, that I may find joy in following you. Emmanuel, bring me abundant life.

Ponder Today

How has this Christmas season shaped me, and what do I want to carry with me into ordinary time?

Prayer for Evening

Jesus, our beginning and end, you come to share every part of being human, and you destroyed the power of sin and death. Grant that I may find joy in following you to new life. Emmanuel, bring me abundant joy.

https://www.avemariapress.com/let-heaven-and-nature-sing-music.

Complete Lyrics

First Week of Advent

Sunday, December 1, through Saturday, December 7

O Come, O Come, Emmanuel

Traditional | Translator: J. M. Neale

O come, O come, Emmanuel, and ransom captive Israel
that mourns in lonely exile here until the Son of God appear.

Refrain:
Rejoice! Rejoice! Emmanuel shall come to you, O Israel.

O come, O Wisdom from on high, who ordered all things mightily;
to us the path of knowledge show and teach us in its ways to go. *Refrain*

O come, O come, great Lord of might, who to your tribes on Sinai's height
in ancient times did give the law, in cloud and majesty and awe. *Refrain*

O come, O Branch of Jesse's stem, unto your own and rescue them!
From depths of hell your people save, and give them victory o'er the grave.
Refrain

O come, O Key of David, come and open wide our heavenly home.
Make safe for us the heavenward road and bar the way to death's abode. *Refrain*

O come, O Bright and Morning Star, and bring us comfort from afar!
Dispel the shadows of the night and turn our darkness into light. *Refrain*

O come, O King of nations, bind in one the hearts of all mankind.
Bid all our sad divisions cease and be yourself our King of Peace. *Refrain*

SECOND WEEK OF ADVENT

Sunday, December 8, and Monday, December 9

AVE MARIA (HAIL MARY)
Traditional

Ave Maria, gratia plena,
Dominus tecum. Benedicta tu in mulieribus,
et benedictus fructus ventris tui, Jesus.

Sancta Maria, Mater Dei,
ora pro nobis peccatoribus,
nunc et in hora mortis nostrae.
Amen.

Hail Mary, full of grace,
the Lord is with you. Blessed are you among women,
and blessed is the fruit of your womb, Jesus.

Holy Mary, Mother of God,
pray for us sinners,
now and at the hour of our death.
Amen.

Tuesday, December 10, and Wednesday, December 11

THE KING SHALL COME WHEN MORNING DAWNS
Author: John Brownlie

The King shall come when morning dawns and light triumphant breaks,
when beauty gilds the eastern hills and life to joy awakes.

Not as of old a little child, to bear, and fight, and die,
but crowned with glory like the sun that lights the morning sky.

O brighter than the rising morn when He, victorious, rose
and left the lonesome place of death, despite the rage of foes.

O brighter than that glorious morn shall this fair morning be,
when Christ, our King, in beauty comes, and we His face shall see.

The King shall come when morning dawns and earth's dark night is past;
O haste the rising of that morn, the day that aye shall last.

And let the endless bliss begin, by weary saints foretold,
when right shall triumph over wrong, and truth shall be extolled.

The King shall come when morning dawns, and light and beauty brings;
"Hail, Christ the Lord!" Thy people pray, come quickly, King of kings!

Thursday, December 12

LA GUADALUPANA (THE VIRGIN OF GUADALUPE)
Traditional

*Desde el cielo, una hermosa mañana, desde el cielo, una hermosa mañana,
la Guadalupana, la Guadalupana, la Guadalupana, bajó al Tepeyac.*

*Su llegada llenó de alegría, su llegada llenó de alegría,
de luz y armonía, de luz y armonía, de luz y armonía, todo el Anáhuac.*

*Por el monte pasaba Juan Diego, por el monte pasaba Juan Diego,
y acercose luego, y acercose luego, y acercose luego al oir cantar.*

*"Juan Dieguito" la Virgen le dijo, "Juan Dieguito" la Virgen le dijo,
"este cerro elijo, este cerro elijo, "este cerro elijo, para hacer mi altar."*

*Suplicante juntaba Sus manos, suplicante juntaba Sus manos,
y eran mexicanos, eran mexicanos, y eran mexicanos Su porte y Su faz.*

*Y en la tilma entre rosas pintada, y en la tilma entre rosas pintada,
su imagen amada, Su imagen amada, su imagen amada, Se dignó dejar.*

*Desde entonces para el Mexicano, desde entonces para el Mexicano,
ser Guadalupano, ser Guadalupano, ser Guadalupano es algo esencial.*

*En sus penas se postran de hinojos, en sus penas se postran de hinojos,
y elevan sus ojos, y elevan sus ojos, y elevan sus ojos, hacia el Tepeyac.*

*Madrecita de los Mexicanos, madrecita de los Mexicanos,
estas en el cielo, estas en el cielo, ruega Dios por nos.*

From heaven on a beautiful morning, from heaven on a beautiful morning,
the Guadalupan Lady, the Guadalupan Lady, the Guadalupan Lady came down
to Tepeyac.

Her arrival filled with happiness, her arrival filled with happiness,
with light and harmony, with light and harmony, with light and harmony, the whole Anáhuac.

By the mountain Juan Diego was passing, by the mountain Juan Diego was passing,
and he approached quickly, approached quickly, he approached quickly when he heard singing.

"Little Juan Diego" the Virgin said, "Little Juan Diego" the Virgin said,
"this hill I choose, this hill I choose, "this hill I choose for my altar to be built."

Pleading She joined her hands, pleading She joined her hands,
they were Mexican, they were Mexican, they were Mexican, Her stance and Her Face.

And on the tilma that was painted among roses, and on the tilma that was painted among roses,
her beloved image, Her beloved image, her beloved image She deigned to leave.

Since then, for the Mexican, since then, for the Mexican,
to be a Guadalupan, to be a Guadalupan, to be a Guadalupan is something essential.

In their sorrows they prostrate on their knees, in their sorrows they prostrate on their knees,
and they raise their eyes, they raise their eyes, and they raise their eyes to Tepeyac.

Dear Mother of the Mexicans, dear Mother of the Mexicans,
you are in Heaven, you are in Heaven, pray to God for us.

Friday, December 13, and Saturday, December 14

DONA NOBIS PACEM (GRANT US PEACE)
Traditional

Dona nobis pacem, pacem.
Dona nobis pacem.

Grant us peace, peace.
Grant us peace.

Third Week of Advent

Sunday, December 15, through Tuesday, December 17

Come, Thou Long-Expected Jesus

Author: Charles Wesley

Come, thou long expected Jesus, born to set thy people free;
from our fears and sins release us, let us find our rest in thee.
Israel's strength and consolation, hope of all the earth thou art;
dear desire of every nation, joy of every longing heart.

Born thy people to deliver, born a child and yet a King,
born to reign in us forever, now thy gracious kingdom bring.
By thine own eternal spirit rule in all our hearts alone;
by thine all sufficient merit, raise us to thy glorious throne.

Wednesday, December 18, through Saturday, December 21

O Come, Divine Messiah

Author: M. l'abbé Pellegrin | Translator: Sister Mary of St. Philip

O come, divine Messiah; the world in silence waits the day
when hope shall sing its triumph and sadness flee away.

Refrain:
Dear Savior, haste! Come, come to earth. Dispel the night and show your face,
and bid us hail the dawn of grace. O come, divine Messiah;
the world in silence waits the day when hope shall sing its triumph
and sadness flee away.

O Christ, whom nations sigh for, whom priest and prophet long foretold,
come, break the captive's fetters, redeem the long-lost fold. *Refrain*

You come in peace and meekness and lowly will your cradle be;
all clothed in human weakness shall we your Godhead see. *Refrain*

FOURTH WEEK OF ADVENT

Sunday, December 22, and Monday, December 23

CREATOR OF THE STARS OF NIGHT

Translator: J. M. Neale

Creator of the stars of night,
your people's everlasting light,
O Christ, Redeemer of us all,
we pray you, hear us when we call.

In sorrow that the ancient curse
should doom to death a universe,
you came to save a ruined race
with healing gifts of heav'nly grace.

When earth drew on to darkest night,
you came, but not in splendor bright,
not as a king, but the child
of Mary, virgin mother mild.

At your great name, majestic now,
all knees must bend, all hearts must bow;
all things on earth with one accord
join those in heav'n to call you Lord.

To God the Father, God the Son,
and God the Spirit, Three in One,
praise, honor, might, and glory be
from age to age eternally.

SILENT NIGHT

Author: Joseph Mohr | Translator: J. Freeman Young

Silent night! Holy night!
All is calm, all is bright
'round yon virgin mother and child!
Holy infant, so tender and mild,
sleep in heavenly peace, sleep in heavenly peace.

Silent night! Holy night!
Shepherds quake at the sight.
Glories stream from heaven afar,
heav'nly hosts sing, "Alleluia!
Christ the Savior is born!
Christ the Savior is born!"

Silent night! Holy night!
Son of God, love's pure light
radiant beams from Thy holy face
with the dawn of redeeming grace,
Jesus, Lord, at Thy birth!
Jesus, Lord, at Thy birth!

Silent night! Holy night!
Wondrous star, lend thy light;
with the angels let us sing
"Alleluia" to our King:
"Christ the Savior is born!
Christ the Savior is born!"

OCTAVE OF CHRISTMAS

Wednesday, December 25, and Thursday, December 26

JOY TO THE WORLD

Author: Isaac Watts

Joy to the world, the Lord is come! Let earth receive her King!
Let every heart prepare him room, and heav'n and nature sing,
and heav'n and nature sing, and heav'n, and heav'n and nature sing.

Joy to the earth, the Savior reigns! Let men their songs employ,
while fields and floods, rocks, hills, and plains repeat the sounding joy,
repeat the sounding joy, repeat, repeat the sounding joy.

No more let sins and sorrows grow, nor thorns infest the ground;
He comes to make his blessings flow far as the curse is found,
far as the curse is found, far as, far as the curse is found.

He rules the world with truth and grace, and makes the nations prove
the glories of his righteousness and wonders of his love,
and wonders of his love, and wonders, wonders of his love.

Friday, December 27, and Saturday, December 28

HARK THE HERALD ANGELS SING

Authors: Charles Wesley, George Whitefield

Hark! the herald angels sing, "Glory to the newborn King:
peace on earth, and mercy mild, God and sinners reconciled!"
Joyful, all ye nations, rise, join the triumph of the skies;
with th'angelic hosts proclaim, "Christ is born in Bethlehem!"
Hark! the herald angels sing, "Glory to the newborn King."

Christ, by highest heaven adored, Christ, the everlasting Lord,
late in time behold him come, offspring of the Virgin's womb:
veiled in flesh the Godhead see; hail th'incarnate Deity,
pleased with us in flesh to dwell, Jesus, our Immanuel.
Hark! the herald angels sing, "Glory to the newborn King."

Hail the heaven-born Prince of Peace! Hail the Sun of Righteousness!
Light and life to all he brings, risen with healing in his wings.
Mild he lays his glory by, born that we no more may die,
born to raise us from the earth, born to give us second birth.
Hark! the herald angels sing, "Glory to the newborn King."

Sunday, December 29, and Monday, December 30

WHAT CHILD IS THIS?
Author: W. Chatterton Dix

What Child is this, who, laid to rest, on Mary's lap is sleeping?
Whom angels greet with anthems sweet, while shepherds watch are keeping?

Refrain:
This, this is Christ, the King, whom shepherds guard and angels sing:
haste, haste to bring Him laud, the Babe, the Son of Mary!

Why lies He in such mean estate, where ox and ass are feeding?
Good Christian, fear: for sinners here the silent Word is pleading. *Refrain*

So bring Him incense, gold, and myrrh, come, peasant, king to own Him.
The King of kings salvation brings; let loving hearts enthrone Him. *Refrain*

Tuesday, December 31, and Wednesday, January 1

THERE IS NO ROSE OF SUCH VIRTUE
Traditional

There is no rose of such virtue as is the rose that bare Jesu; alleluia.
For in this rose contained was heaven and earth in little space;
res miranda [a thing to be wondered at].
By that rose we may well see that He is God in persons three,
pari forma [equal in form].

The angels sang the shepherds to: *gloria in excelsis Deo*:
gaudeamus [Glory to God in the highest: let us rejoice].
Now leave we all this worldly mirth and follow we this joyful birth;
transeamus [let us pass over].

CHRISTMAS SEASON

Thursday, January 2, through Saturday, January 4
O COME, ALL YE FAITHFUL
Author: John Francis Wade | Translator: Frederick Oakeley

O come, all ye faithful, joyful and triumphant,
O come ye, O come ye to Bethlehem!
Come, and behold him, born the King of angels!

Refrain:
O come, let us adore him;
O come, let us adore him;
O come, let us adore him, Christ, the Lord!

God of God, Light of Light,
lo, he abhors not the virgin's womb;
very God, begotten not created; *Refrain*

Sing, choirs of angels; sing in exultation;
sing, all ye citizens of heav'n above!
Glory to God, all glory in the highest! *Refrain*

Yea, Lord, we greet thee, born this happy morning;
Jesus, to Thee be all glory giv'n!
Word of the Father, now in flesh appearing! *Refrain*

Sunday, January 5, and Monday, January 6
WE THREE KINGS OF ORIENT ARE
Author: John H. Hopkins

We three kings of Orient are;
bearing gifts we traverse afar,
field and fountain, moor and mountain,
following yonder star.

Refrain:
O star of wonder, star of light,
star with royal beauty bright,

westward leading, still proceeding,
guide us to thy perfect light.

Born a King on Bethlehem's plain,
gold I bring to crown him again,
King forever, ceasing never,
over us all to reign. *Refrain*

Frankincense to offer have I;
incense owns a Deity nigh;
prayer and praising, voices raising,
worshiping God on high. *Refrain*

Myrrh is mine; its bitter perfume
breathes a life of gathering gloom;
sorrowing, sighing, bleeding, dying,
sealed in the stone-cold tomb. *Refrain*

Glorious now behold him arise;
King and God and sacrifice:
Alleluia, Alleluia,
sounds through the earth and skies. *Refrain*

Tuesday, January 7, and Wednesday, January 8

THE FIRST NOEL

Anonymous

The first Noel the angel did say
was to certain poor shepherds in fields as they lay,
in fields where they lay keeping their sheep,
on a cold winter's night that was so deep.

Refrain:
Noel, Noel, Noel, Noel
born is the King of Israel.

They looked up and saw a star
shining in the east beyond them far;
and to the earth it gave great light,
and so it continued both day and night. *Refrain*

And by the light of that same star
three wise men came from country far;
to seek for a king was their intent,
and to follow the star wherever it went. *Refrain*

This star drew nigh to the northwest;
o'er Bethlehem it took its rest,
and there it did both stop and stay,
right over the place where Jesus lay. *Refrain*

Then entered in those wise men three,
full reverently upon their knee,
and offered there in his presence
their gold, and myrrh, and frankincense. *Refrain*

Then let us all with one accord sing
praises to our heavenly Lord,
that hath made heaven and earth of nought,
and with his blood our life hath bought. *Refrain*

Thursday, January 9, and Friday, January 10

O HOLY NIGHT

Author: Placide Cappeau | Translator: John S. Dwight

O holy night! the stars are brightly shining;
it is the night of the dear Savior's birth.
Long lay the world in sin and error pining,
till He appeared and the soul felt its worth.
A thrill of hope—the weary world rejoices,
for yonder breaks a new and glorious morn!
Fall on your knees! O hear the angel voices!
O night divine, O night when Christ was born!
O night, O holy night, O night divine!

Led by the light of faith serenely beaming,
with glowing hearts by his cradle we stand.
So led by light of a star sweetly gleaming,
here came the Wise Men from Orient land.
The King of kings lay thus in lowly manger,
in all our trials born to be our Friend.

He knows our need—to our weakness is no stranger.
Behold your King, before Him lowly bend!
Behold your King, before Him lowly bend!

Truly He taught us to love one another;
his law is love and His gospel is peace.
Chains shall He break, for the slave is our brother,
and in His name all oppression shall cease.
Sweet hymns of joy in grateful chorus raise we;
let all within us praise His holy name.
Christ is the Lord! O praise His name forever!
His pow'r and glory evermore proclaim!
His pow'r and glory evermore proclaim!

Saturday, January 11, and Monday, January 12

GO TELL IT ON THE MOUNTAIN
Adapter: John W. Work

Refrain:
Go tell it on the mountain,
over the hills, and ev'rywhere;
go, tell it on the mountain
that Jesus Christ is born.

While shepherds kept their watching
o'er silent flocks by night,
behold, throughout the heavens
there shone a holy light. *Refrain*

The shepherds feared and trembled
when lo, above the earth
rang out the angel chorus
that hailed our Savior's birth. *Refrain*

Down in a lowly manger
the humble Christ was born,
and God sent us salvation
that blessed Christmas morn. *Refrain*

Founded in 1865 by Fr. Edward Sorin, CSC, **Ave Maria Press** is an apostolate of the Congregation of Holy Cross, United States Province of Priests and Brothers. Ave is a nonprofit Catholic publishing ministry that serves the spiritual and formative needs of the Church and its schools, institutions, and ministers; Christian individuals and families; and others seeking spiritual nourishment.

Ave remains one of the oldest continually operating Catholic publishing houses in the country and a leader in publishing Catholic high school religion textbooks, ministry resources, and books on prayer and spirituality.

In the tradition of Holy Cross, Ave is committed, as an educator in the faith, to help people know, love, and serve God and to spread the gospel of Jesus Christ through books and other resources.

Ave Maria Press perpetuates Fr. Sorin's vision to honor Mary and provide an important outlet for good Catholic writing.

Josh Noem is the editorial director at Ave Maria Press. He began his writing career as a Catholic journalist and served as editor of the FaithND and Grotto Network platforms before joining Ave in 2022. His book, *The End of Ending*, was recognized as one of the best Catholic novels of 2021. Noem grew up in the Black Hills of South Dakota and earned a master of divinity degree from the University of Notre Dame.

Noem and his family live in South Bend, Indiana.

Instagram: @Josh Noem
joshnoem.substack.com

Listen to the carols and hymns mentioned throughout *Let Heaven and Nature Sing* all in one place!

Scan the QR code above or visit
avemariapress.com/let-heaven-and-nature-sing-music